MY FIRST
GREECE

CW00853209

ALL ABOUT GREECE FOR KIDS

GL BED
CHILDREN BOOKS

Copyright 2023 by Globed Children Books
All rights reserved. No part of this book may be reproduced or distributed in any form without prior written permission from the author, with the exception of non-commercial uses permitted by copyright law.
Limited of Liability/Disclaimer of Warranty: The publisher and author make no representations or liabilities with respect to the accuracy and completeness of the contents of this work and specifically disclaim all warranties including without limitations warranties of fitness of particular purpose. No warranty may be created or extended by sales or promotional materials. This work is sold with the understanding that the publisher and author is not engaging in rendering medical, legal or any other professional advice or service. Further, readers should be aware that websites listed in this work may have changed or disappeared between when this work was written and when it is read.

Interior and cover Design: Daniel Day
Editor: Margaret Bam

For My Sons, Daniel, David and Jude

Church in Santorini, Greece

Greece

Greece is a **country**.

A country is land that is controlled by a **single government**. Countries are also called **nations, states, or nation-states**.

Countries can be **different sizes**. Some countries are big and others are small.

Parthenon. Greece

Where Is Greece?

Greece is located in the continent of **Europe.**

A continent is **a massive area of land that is separated from others by water or other natural features**.

Greece is situated in Southern Europe.

Athens, Greece

Capital

The capital of Greece is **Athens**.

Athens is located in the **southern part** of the country.

Athens is the largest city in Greece.

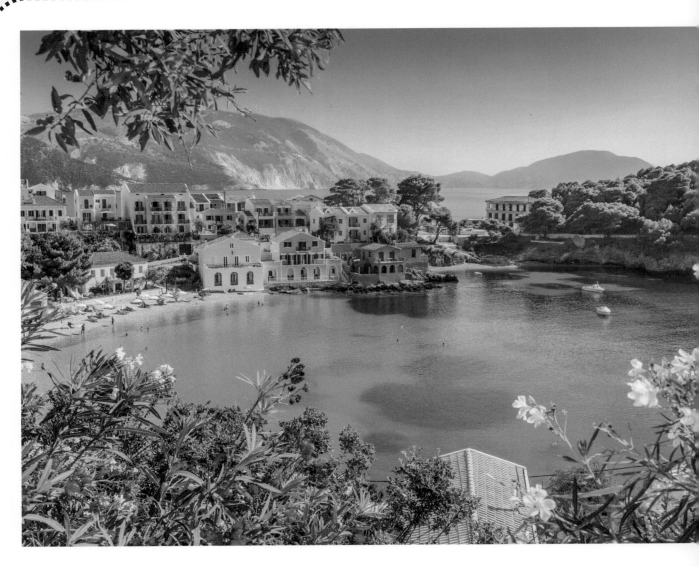

Kefalonia, Greece

Regions

Greece is a country that is made up of 13 regions and 1 autonomous region.

The regions of Greece are as follows:

Attica, Central Greece, Central Macedonia, Crete, Eastern Macedonia and Thrace, Epirus, Ionian Islands, North Aegean, Peloponnese, South Aegean, Thessaly, Western Greece, Western Macedonia and Monastic community of Mount Athos.

Mykonos, Greece

Population

Greece has population of around **10 million people** making it the 88th most populated country in the world and the 13th most populated country in Europe.

Size

Greece is **131,957 square kilometres** making it the 15th largest country in Europe by area.

Greece is the 95th largest country in the world.

Languages

The official language of Greece is **Greek**. The Greek language originated in Greece and holds a very important place in the history of the Western world.

Here are a few Greek phrases
- **Γειά σου** - Hello
- **Χάρηκα πολύ** - Nice to meet you
- **Τι κανείς** - How are you?
- **Ευχαριστώ** - Thank you

Athens, Grece

Attractions

There are lots of interesting places to see in Greece.

Some beautiful places to visit in Greece are

- **Meteora**
- **Acropolis of Athens**
- **Parthenon**
- **Acropolis Museum**
- **Archaeological site of Mycenae**
- **Archaeological Site of Olympia**

Corfu, Greece

History of Greece

People have lived in Greece for a very long time. It is believed that humans have inhabited Greece from as early as 270,000 BC.

Greece is the birthplace of the first advanced civilizations in Europe and is considered to be the birthplace of Western civilisation.

Assos Village, Kefalonia, Greece

Customs in Greece

Greece has many fascinating customs and traditions.

- **It is common for Greek children to stay in their parents home until they get married.**
- **Greeks are very family orientated and it is common for elders to move back in with their children or grandchildren to stay with them for their final years.**

Symi, Greece

Music of Greece

There are many different music genres in Greece such as **Greek operetta, Rebetiko, Éntekhno, Laïkó, Modern laïká and Skyládiko.**

Some notable Greek musicians include
- **Demis Roussos**
- **Mikis Theodorakis**
- **George Dalaras**
- **Anna Vissi**
- **Marinella**
- **Haris Alexiou**

Moussaka

Food of Greece

Greece is known for its delicious, flavoursome and diverse food.

The national dish of Greece is **Moussaka** which is a hearty casserole made with eggplants and minced meat.

Food of Greece

Some popular dishes in Greece include

- **Taramasalata**
- **Papoutsakia**
- **Pastitsio**
- **Souvlaki**
- **Stifado**
- **Soutzoukakia**
- **Tomatokeftedes**

Corfu, Greece

Weather in Greece

Greece has a Mediterranean climate, with mild and wet winters and hot, dry summers.

The warmest months are **July and August.**

Meteora, Greece

Animals of Greece

There are many wonderful animals in Greece.

Here are some animals that live in Greece

- **Boar**
- **Martens**
- **Bears**
- **Wolves**
- **Lynxes**

Zakynthos Island, Greece

Beaches

There are many beautiful beaches in Greece which is one of the reasons why so many people visit this beautiful country every year.

Here are some of Greece's beaches

- **Elafonissi**
- **Plaka Beach**
- **Platys Gialos**
- **Ornos Beach**
- **Faragas Beach**

Naxos, Greece

Sports of Greece

Sports play an integral part in Greek culture. The most popular sport is **Football.**

Here are some of famous sportspeople from Greece

- **Giannis Antetokounmpo - Basketball**
- **Ekaterini Thanou - Athletics**
- **Katerina Stefanidi - Athletics**
- **Stefanos Tsitsipas - Tennis**

Patmos Island, Greece

Famous

Many successful people hail from Greece.

Here are some notable Greek figures

- **Maria Callas – Singer**
- **Archimedes – Mathematician**
- **Nikos Kazantzakis – Writer**
- **Homer – Poet**
- **Pericles – Politician**

Santorini Island, Greece

Something Extra...

As a little something extra, we are going to share some lesser known facts about Greece.

- Greek is the world's oldest language that is still in use.
- The yoyo was created in Greece.
- Greece is the third biggest producer of olive oil in the world.

Words From the Author

We hope that you enjoyed learning about the wonderful country of Greece.

Greece is a country rich in culture and beauty, with lots of wonderful places to visit and people to meet.

We hope you continue to learn more about this wonderful nation. If you enjoyed this book, consider leaving a review!

With Love

Printed in Great Britain
by Amazon

23474728R10027